First published in Great Britain in 2002 by Brimax,
an imprint of Octopus Publishing Group Ltd
2-4 Heron Quays, London E14 4JP

Created by Nimbus Books
Written by Lynne Gibbs
Illustrated by John Eastwood
Edited in the U.S. by Joanna Schmalz, Lindsay Mizer, and Tracy Paulus

Mc Graw Hill **Children's Publishing**

This edition published in the United States of America in 2003 by
McGraw-Hill Children's Publishing,
a Division of The McGraw-Hill Companies
8787 Orion Place
Columbus, Ohio 43240-4027

www.MHkids.com

Library of Congress Cataloging-in-Publication Data is on file with the publisher.

Printed in China.

1-57768-556-3

1 2 3 4 5 6 7 8 9 10 BRI 09 08 07 06 05 04 03 02

The McGraw-Hill Companies

Don't Slurp Your Soup!

Contents

Good manners

Why are good manners so important? Well, unless you live on the moon or in a deep, dark forest, you will see other people everyday. So, it is important for us to get along with each other.

What are good manners?

Is it enough to know which utensil to use or how to write a thank you letter? Not quite. You also need to show consideration for other people and think carefully about how your actions will affect them.

Thanks, Mom!

The people who care for you spend a lot of time making sure you have all the love and attention you need. Why not show them how much you care, too, by giving them a big hug and saying *thank you*?

Being polite and thoughtful

If you behave badly toward someone, he or she will feel miserable. So, the next time you are tempted to forget your manners, stop and think for a second. Always try to be polite, thoughtful, and caring. You will be a much happier person and so will others!

The benefits of good manners

If you have good manners, people will like being around you. And let's face it, we all enjoy company. There's nothing better than feeling that our friends and family enjoy being around us.

Also, if you show that you care about other people, they will likely behave the same way toward you. Soon, you will find that you have more friends and lots more people offering to do nice things for you, too. Now that can't be bad, can it?

Kate and her brother Tom are going to help us learn about good manners.

The magic words

Let's start with the basics. You already know how to say *please*, *thank you*, and *you're welcome*. You'll be surprised by how much these little words mean.

Please

"I want a vanilla ice cream cone!" Now what kind of way is that to ask for something, hmm? Let's start again.

"*Please* may I have a vanilla ice cream cone?" Perfect! Now you have what you wanted, and the clerk is happy. In fact, she even smiles as she hands you your cone!

Always ask with a *please*

So, the rule is whenever you are asking for something, start your sentence with the word *please*. You will be amazed by how many people are impressed by your good manners.

Thank you

But wait a minute! When the clerk gives you your ice cream, you take it and walk out of the store without another word! Come back inside and see what you have forgotten. When you took your ice cream cone from the clerk, you should have said *thank you*.

You're welcome

You said the word *please* before asking for something, and then you said *thank you* when taking it. But now it's the clerk's turn to say something. When a person says *thank you*, it is polite for you to then add *you're welcome*.

So remember:

• *Please* when you want something.

• *Thank you* when you get it.

• *You're welcome* when someone thanks you.

• Even if someone else forgets their manners, you should respond politely to their request.

Table manners

Having good table manners is important. After all, there is nothing worse than listening to someone slurping, burping, and sucking their way through a meal. So, here is what you should do.

Sticky fingers

We eat most food with utensils, but there are some foods that even your mom will let you eat with your fingers. These include sandwiches, potato chips, corn on the cob, and fruit.

dessert spoon

dessert fork

bread knife

napkin

fork

plate

side dish

Utensil confusion!

You've been invited out for a fancy meal, but when you see all the utensils, you break into a sweat. Just which knife, fork, and spoon are you supposed to use first? Simple, start with the utensil placed on the outside, and course by course, work inward, then upward.

Napkins

This *may come* as a surprise, but a napkin is not for blowing your nose or hiding unwanted vegetables. It is for dabbing your lips! When you sit down, unfold your napkin and lay it across your lap.

knife

glass

soup
spoon

Take a break!

You are not a hamster, so do not stuff food into your mouth until your cheeks are bulging. Take short pauses, placing your utensils apart at a slight angle on the plate. Once you have finished eating, lay the knife and fork (or fork and spoon) side by side, with the prongs of the fork pointing upward.

Ultimate NO-NOs

Things you should NEVER, EVER do at the table:

- Take food from your neighbor's plate.

- Pick food out of your teeth with your fingernail.

11

Being respectful

If you treat other people the way you would like them to treat you, you will not go wrong. Good manners are all about thinking of other people and being respectful.

Do not interrupt

It is rude to interrupt when someone is speaking, so wait until the person has finished before you butt in! If you need to speak to someone urgently (and "urgent" doesn't mean asking someone if they are going to finish their fries!), gently put your hand on her arm and say, "*I'm sorry* to interrupt, but could I speak to you, please?"

Sharing is caring

Just because Aunt Alice has given you a huge box of chocolates, it does not mean you have to hog them all to yourself! Offer them to others! It would be a nice gesture if you offered them around BEFORE eating all your favorite ones! If you share your things with others, they will want to share their things with you, too!

Practice patience

No one likes it when someone cuts into a line, so be patient and wait your turn. It can be scary, especially for elderly people, when kids shove each other to be first in line. You may think you are only having fun, but other people may not agree.

Respect for others

If you push, shove, shout, interrupt, and refuse to share anything, why should others treat you with respect? The next time you forget where you left your manners, apologize and try to make up for your rudeness.

Ultimate NO-NOs

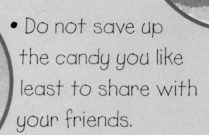

• Never shove someone out of the way to get the last seat on the bus.

• Do not save up the candy you like least to share with your friends.

• Never yawn or tap your feet impatiently if you are bored by someone's conversation.

Everyday manners

Let's be honest. We all do it—burp, pass gas, and sneeze that is.
How many of us can say we have never, ever picked our noses?
But there is a time and a place for everything.

Nose picking

If your nostrils need clearing,
USE A TISSUE! Do not wipe your nose
on your sleeve, the tablecloth, or your
best friend's coat!

Burping

You may feel better by burping loudly, especially after eating or drinking, but other people around you will not! If you cannot stop a burp from bursting out, then cover your mouth with your hand and say *excuse me* afterward.

Passing gas

Now, how can I put this politely? Let's say that you need to pass gas. What do you do? Letting it out and blaming the dog is NOT the answer! Go somewhere private, and then let it out. If you accidentally pass gas in company, do not blame the person standing next to you. Own up and say *excuse me.*

Ultimate NO-NOs

Things you should NEVER, EVER do:

• Examine, or even eat, the contents of your nose.

• Sneeze, cough, or yawn without covering your mouth.

• Burp, even quietly, in someone's face.

Coughs and sneezes

Some people sneeze quietly, while others give great, big, hurricane-style sneezes! Whichever way you sneeze, HOLD A TISSUE OVER YOUR MOUTH. Other people do not want whatever is up your nose to be sprayed all over them! Sneezing and coughing are the fastest ways to spread germs.

Introductions

How do you introduce people? It is no use just saying, "Mom, this is Andy," because your mom will not know if Andy is a friend, neighbor, or someone you found in your closet!

What's your name?

It can be difficult to know how to introduce family members, especially to a younger person. Do you say, "Mom, this is my friend, Andy. Andy, this is my mom, Mrs. Sanders." Or do you introduce your mom by her first name? To save embarrassment, ask your parents in advance how they prefer to be introduced.

Something in common

When you introduce people to each other, adding extra information such as where they are from, their job, or even their hobby can be helpful. This gives people something to talk to each other about.

Golden rules

If you remember two things, introductions will be simple:

• Always use both people's names twice. "Lexi, this is Allison. Allison, this is Lexi."

• Begin with the names of older people, women, high-ranking and important people, such as teachers, politicians, clergymen, and celebrities.

Proper forms of address

If you are introducing an older person or someone in authority, such as a teacher, you would say, "Mr. Mason, may I introduce my friend, Andy? Andy, this is my teacher, Mr. Mason." If someone has a title, always use it. For example, "Father Callihan, may I introduce General Johnson? General Johnson, this is Father Callihan."

Ultimate NO-NOs

Things you should NEVER do when introducing people:

• Get someone's name wrong.

• Only give one person's name.

Letter writing

There are many ways to keep in touch with people. Writing letters is one of them. Different kinds of letters need to be written in different ways. Here are two examples.

The date goes here.

The greeting shows who is receiving the letter.

July 24, 2003

Dear Mary,

   It was really nice to see you last we[ek?] I had a great time at Susan's party a[nd] hope you did as well. I liked playing games and meeting Bonzo, the funny clown best.

   I know your mom had a very long [drive] home after the party, so I hope you didn't get to bed too late!

   Don't forget that we have both been invited to Janet's party next Saturday. I can hardly wait!

Love,

Kate

Kate

Put your letter in paragraphs.

A friendly letter

Your address goes here.

The recipient's address goes here.

Kate Barker
35 Maple Street
Thornton, MA
01749

Mary Sullivan
102 Hope Avenue
Providence, RI
01245

Addressing an envelope

   Write your address in the upper left-hand corner of the envelope. If there is a problem delivering the letter, then it will be returned to you. You can write the name of the state or use its abbreviation.

A formal letter

The address of the person receiving the letter goes below the date.

If you can find out the name of the person you are writing to, put his or her name in the greeting.

Choose a formal closing.

Use your first and last names in your signature.

Tom Barker
35 Maple Street
Thornton, MA 01749

August 28, 2002

Readers Book Shop
23 Main Street
Thornton, MA 01749

Dear Sir or Madam,

   I am trying to purchase a book entitled How to Eat Without Dribbling. I wonder if you would be kind enough to let me know if you have a copy of this book for sale in your book shop?

   I have enclosed a self-addressed stamped envelope for y

Sincerely yours,

Tom Barker
Tom Barker

Your address goes here, so the person receiving the letter knows where to send the reply.

Use a polite tone and straightforward facts in your letter.

Don't forget the stamp!

   Make sure you put enough stamps on your envelope. If you don't, the letter will be returned, and you will have to pay the extra postage.

Phones and e-mail

Thanks to the telephone and e-mail, we can contact almost anyone in an instant! But remember, your voice and e-mail may be the only impression a person gets of you. That's why telephone and e-mail manners are very important.

Telephone tips

Before making a call, turn off anything that makes background noises like the television or radio. When someone answers, give your name and the reason that you are calling. If the person you are calling sounds busy, ask if you can call back another time. Do not eat or drink while you are using the telephone.

E-mails

Sending e-mails lets other people reply at a time that is convenient for them. Adding a smiley face is a sure way to cheer up friends! :) But remember, teasing doesn't come across in e-mails, so avoid it. Try not to use bold type or all capital letters—it comes across as if you are shouting . Also, don't send big files without permission—it can make some computers crash.

Cell phones

Cell phones are convenient, but they can sometimes bother other people. Always turn off your cell phone whenever you are:

• Inside a public building, such as a hospital, doctor's office, library, cinema, church, or at school!

• Speaking to other people.

Messages

Keep a notepad and pencil near your telephone so that you can take messages. If you leave a message, clearly give your name, telephone number, and a time when you can be reached.

Ultimate NO-NOs

Things you should NEVER do on the phone:

• Call someone in the morning or late at night, unless you have been asked to or it is an emergency.

• Shout and laugh loudly into your cell phone when you are in public places.

21

Being a good host

Good manners are the key to a successful party! Make sure that you are a polite and respectful host. Check that there is enough food and drinks for everyone and plenty of games to play.

Sending invitations

There is no point having a party if you do not tell anyone about it! Make a list of people you would like to invite. Then send out invitations. They shouldn't be distributed anywhere people might get their feelings hurt if they're not invited.

What an invitation needs to say

An invitation needs to give the following information:

• Why you are having a party. Is it to celebrate your birthday, Christmas, Halloween, or something else?

• Your name, contact address, and telephone number.

• Where your party is being held.

• The date and time of the party.

You are invited to a birthday party

for Tom Barker

on Saturday, June 20

at 4:00 pm

at 35 Maple Street

Thornton, MA 01749

R.S.V.P.
Tom Barker 555 – 1234

Thank you notes

After a party, it is always polite to write a note to the host, thanking him or her for inviting you. (And that means even if it was the worst party you have EVER been to!) If you were the host and received presents, thank you notes are a definite must. Write down who each gift is from so you can include a peronal thank you in your thank you note.

R.S.V.P.

To make sure people reply, telling you whether they can come to your party or not, write *R.S.V.P.* These letters stand for "Répondez, s'il vous plaît," the French words for "Reply, if you please."

Ultimate NO-NOs

Things you should NEVER, EVER do at a party:

• Forget to reply to your invitation and just show up.

• Uninvite someone to your party.

• Discuss a party in front of people who have not been invited.

Party manners

Whether you are giving a party or just going to one, it is important to remember your manners. Even on relaxed occasions such as parties, people will notice how you behave.

Being a good guest

The first sign of good manners is to arrive on time! A party is a time to have fun but that does not mean at the expense of everyone else. Don't show off or try to be the center of attention.

Respect your host

Wait for the host to tell everyone when it's time to eat, rather than gobbling all the food on your own. If you are being served something you don't care for, politely say, *no, thank you*, and choose something else to eat.

Being a good host

Make guests feel welcome by introducing them to each other. You will need to make sure they have enough food and drinks throughout the party, too.

Any special requests?

If you have invited someone who has special needs, plan ahead and make sure you have provided for their needs. A vegetarian will appreciate it if you have special food for him. A friend in a wheelchair may need help getting up stairs.

Party clothes

You should always state on invitations what kind of party you are giving. Is it a formal, informal, or even a costume party? People will be embarrassed if they show up in a formal outfit when everyone else is wearing jeans!

Ultimate NO-NOs

Things you should NEVER do at a party:

- Have a food fight with the leftovers.

- Overeat and make yourself sick.

- Leave without thanking the host.

- Say *yuck* if you receive a gift you do not care for.

Being a good sport

After a game, how often have you heard someone say, "It's not whether you win or lose, it's how you play the game!"? If you take part in any game, you should always play fairly and be a good sport.

Being a good sport

Do not lose your temper or shout at the person or team you are playing against. Show you are prepared to lose as well as win a game and be a good sport about it. Never argue with a referee, They are only doing their job. At the end of the game, smile and shake hands with your opponent(s).

Cheating

Even if you know that you are not as good as the other player, do not be tempted to cheat. Just do the best you can and remember that every time you play, you will gain more experience and become better at that game. Cheaters are nearly always caught. Then you would feel really silly, wouldn't you?

Team player

If you are playing on a team, do not try to take over the game! You may think you are the best player ever, but as part of a team, you all need to work together, each using your best skills.

Good spectators

Good sportsmanship should extend to the sidelines, too. If you're watching a game, don't be tempted to cheer when a contestant makes a mistake. And never shout out rude comments about your team's opponents or boo them!

Ultimate NO-NOs

Things you should NEVER do when playing a game:

- Trip someone on purpose.

- Refuse to shake hands when you lose.

- Call your opponent names to discourage or distract him.

Out and about

No matter how bright or funny you are, if you do not know how to behave properly, most people will remember your bad manners!

After you

Holding a door open for someone else to go through first shows good manners. That does not mean you have to hold open a door until a long line of shoppers has passed through! But if there are only a few people, hold open the door and politely say *after you*.

What's the rush?

Running up or down stairs can be dangerous. You could trip and fall or cause someone else to have an accident. Watch out for others, and walk around people carrying lots of bags or young children.